Original title:
In the Orchard's Shadow

Copyright © 2025 Creative Arts Management OÜ
All rights reserved.

Author: Julian Carmichael
ISBN HARDBACK: 978-1-80566-655-4
ISBN PAPERBACK: 978-1-80566-940-1

Veils of Lush Green

Chasing after apples, I took a fall,
Only to find a worm, having a ball.
Laughter echoes through branches above,
As a squirrel mocks me, the fruit of love.

Bees buzzing loudly, thinking they're slick,
I dodge and weave, but oh, what a trick!
With each sticky splash, my hair turns bright,
Nature's own styling; a hilarious sight.

Dappled Light and Hidden Thoughts

Sunlight dances on my nose, oh dear,
A butterfly lands, whispering, 'Stay here.'
But as I do, a bird swipes my hat,
Mocking me softly, that feathered brat!

Under the canopy, I plot my quest,
Just to find snacks and all of the rest.
A picnic awaits, but ants have their say,
Leading the charge, stealing crumbs away.

Beneath the Blooming Canopy

Petals fall down like tiny pink rain,
While I sit here, just looking insane.
A bee steals my drink, oh what a thief,
It waltzes away, leaving me in grief.

A cat jumps out high, causing quite a scene,
Scaring the bunnies, oh, what a routine!
Under the blooms, it's all fun and games,
But in this chase, I forget all my aims.

The Forgotten Pathway

I wander down paths with a curious grin,
Finding lost treasures where mischief begins.
A rubber chicken flops right by my feet,
You'd think in this place, I'd find something sweet!

So I gather the fruit, but oh, what a sight!
Slipping on peels, I take off in flight.
Laughing so hard, I roll in the hay,
In this garden of giggles, I'll forever stay.

A Tapestry of Shadows

Underneath the leafy trees,
Squirrels dance with agile ease.
They steal seeds with cheeky grins,
While tiny birds plot their sins.

The shadows play a game of tag,
While crickets chirp, the frogs all brag.
A breeze whispers through the boughs,
A laugh erupts from nature's prow.

Sunlight dapples through the green,
Wily goats are seldom seen.
They munch leaves and nibble stalks,
While laughing trees converse in talks.

In this realm of laughter's bloom,
Even bugs will find their room.
With every shadow, joy takes flight,
Yonder prickly pear shines bright.

Fruits of Reflection

Peaches roll like laughter's sound,
While cherries tumble on the ground.
A squirrel winks, a prankster bold,
As apples eavesdrop, tales unfold.

A grapevine whispers jokes galore,
While kids giggle and seekers explore.
The sun spills light with a twinkling cue,
As shadows dance in shades of blue.

What's that, a melon in a hat?
Mixed-up fruits, how about that?
The citrus laughs at the apple's plight,
While pumpkins glow in the setting light.

Nature's folly in every piece,
These fruits of joy will never cease.
Their sweetness brings a playful cheer,
As wise old leaves lend us an ear.

Embracing Nature's Embrace

Beneath the boughs, the critters peek,
Where mischief hides and rascals squeak.
A bunny hops with quite the flair,
As butterflies twirl in the air.

The breeze teases the rustling leaves,
With giggles shared by nature's thieves.
Their whispers twine with giggles bright,
As shadows dance in sheer delight.

Odd-shaped pears with caps like hats,
Hosting parties with joyful chats.
A friendly breeze brings nature's song,
As fruit and fun just can't go wrong.

Together we weave a merry tale,
Of playful shadows that never pale.
Let nature's laughter fill the space,
For here we thrive in joy's embrace.

The Poetry of Swaying Limbs

Waving arms of branches high,
A playful dance beneath the sky.
The wind composes funny tunes,
While shadows waltz with daisies' boons.

A citrus sings a silly rhyme,
As dancing limbs keep perfect time.
With every sway, they share a jest,
A sing-song laugh—their very best.

They shake their leaves in joyful ways,
Inviting all to join the play.
With every breeze, the laughter grows,
As swaying limbs put on their shows.

Nature's giggles fill the air,
The boughs all twist, without a care.
A cheerful ruckus joins our path,
In every limb, there's joy and math.

Whispers Beneath the Canopy

The apples giggle in the breeze,
While pears tell secrets with such ease.
A squirrel dances like a clown,
As shadows chase the sunlit brown.

A chubby bee sings off-key tunes,
While plums debate the rise of moons.
The leaves, they chuckle, rustle and sway,
And tickle the toes of the passersby play.

Sunlit Secrets of the Grove

The lemons plot a prank so bold,
While oranges boast of tales retold.
Beneath the stalks, a rabbit sneezes,
And dandelions blow, causing wheezes.

The sun peeks in with a wry smile,
As grapes discuss their latest style.
A cherry bounces, full of cheer,
Its laughter spreads both far and near.

Fruitful Gaze

With brows so furrowed in a fruit war,
The berries argue who can soar.
One claims to fly, the other to float,
While bananas plan a winning coat.

A cantaloupe wears glasses askew,
Declaring itself the scholar of the crew.
With jesters all around to amuse,
No chance of sorrow in this colorful fuse.

Beneath Boughs of Solitude

In solitude, the lemons think,
They ponder life's profound pink drink.
The lonesome kiwis roll their eyes,
As laughter bubbles, oh so wise.

The oranges share a juicy tale,
While at their feet, a snail sets sail.
The fruit debate, each one a star,
In shades of fun, both near and far.

In the Shade of Abundance

Beneath the trees where laughter plays,
Squirrels plot their nutty ways.
Chasing shadows, dodging light,
Who knew that fruit could spark such flight?

Apples giggle, pears take stand,
While cherries play a marching band.
A lemon drops its sour frown,
As oranges roll all over town.

The wind whirls whispers, soft and bright,
As ants parade with tiny might.
Each puddle reflects a jolly cheer,
In this quirky orchard year after year.

And in the breeze, a band plays tunes,
As bees buzz in their golden swoons.
Under canopies of green delight,
The shade invites us, feels so right.

Where Roots Entwine

Roots like dancers twist and turn,
In soil where secrets yearn.
They wiggle waggled, like a rhyme,
Each knot a joke—what a grand time!

Beneath the surface, stories flow,
As gopher giggles, puts on a show.
A worm in shades reads tales so sly,
In the underground where weird dreams fly.

"They found my stash!" the carrots shout,
While turnips hide, full of doubt.
The laughter rolls in earthy beds,
As fungi wear their funny heads.

What a party in the ground,
With moos and oinks, they spin around.
In this quiet nook of pure delight,
Nature's roots know how to excite.

The Language of Blossoms

Tulips tease with vibrant hues,
While daisies dance in morning dew.
Roses wink their fragrant eyes,
While violets plot some silly lies.

Petals whisper in the breeze,
"Let's swap some jokes, if you please!"
The sunflowers bow, then raise their heads,
To echo rhymes the garden spreads.

Bumblebees hum a jazzy beat,
As blooms get up to tap their feet.
With pollen bops and nectar swings,
Each flower knows what humor brings.

In this tangled, cheerful parade,
Laughter blooms where colors played.
With every blossom in fine array,
Nature's giggles light the day.

Etched in Nature's Canvas

On nature's page, a splash of cheer,
Brush strokes of joy through leaves appear.
With colors bright and shapes so round,
Each detail's focus shifts, unbound.

The sunset paints with fuchsia wit,
While clouds above play tag, they flit.
A canvas vast, where moments blend,
In artful mischief, laughs ascend.

A snail in stripes races a hare,
With every move, a joke to share.
Among the brush, a frog recites,
A silly rhyme that sparks delights.

And so the park, a gallery grand,
With nature's humor hand in hand.
Each step a stroke of joyful art,
Where laughter and life never part.

The Harmony of Bursting Buds

Buds break with a creak, like old knees,
Little insects hold crazy parties with ease.
Petals dance like they're on a big stage,
While squirrels debate who's the best sage.

Bees waltz around in a fuzzy parade,
Chasing each other, there's no need for aid.
The wind sings a tune that's sticky-sweet,
As critters hold hands and tap their tiny feet.

Through the Awning of Foliage

Through leaves that wave, I spy a scene,
A raccoon in shades, looking quite keen.
Sipping on nectar, he lets out a sigh,
"Life's just grand when you're too cool to fly."

A lizard joins in, doing the twist,
While worms create tunes that no one can miss.
Best friends forever, at least till the morn,
They giggle and squabble, their laughter reborn.

Whispers Beneath the Boughs

Whispers echo from branches high,
"What's that? A fruit in a tie?"
Apples gossip about the pears,
While lemons joke about their sour affairs.

A chatty little sparrow takes the lead,
"No worms today, only sunshine we need!"
Grapefruits roll over, plotting a prank,
As foliage giggles from its leafy bank.

Secrets of the Fruitful Grove

Secrets hide where the shadows merge,
Cherry trees plot with a flamboyant surge.
"Let's throw a feast," the peaches exclaim,
"Invite the plums, we'll run the same game!"

The cherries arrive with a pop and a bounce,
While lemons lament, searching for a pounce.
Joy spills out, with laughter confined,
Amongst fruity friends, hilarity unwind.

The Glow of Dappled Morn

Sunlight plays in golden beams,
The squirrels dance in silly schemes.
A bird sings songs of lost and found,
While ants march in a jerky round.

Breezes whisper, tickling leaves,
Caught in laughter, time deceives.
A fruit drops low with a gentle thud,
And splat! – the dog's now covered in mud!

Where Time Tangles with Roots

Beneath the boughs, a penny rolls,
The cat heads out, its purpose strolls.
A startled rabbit makes a dash,
While ducks parade in a comical splash.

Knotted roots twist like old tales,
Mixing up with giggles and wails.
A chicken's attempt to fly up high,
Ends with feathers stuck in a pie!

The Allure of Forgotten Fruits

Beneath the tree, a treasure lies,
Green bananas with funny eyes.
They laugh and wiggle, what a sight,
While ants march past on their nightly flight.

An apple claimed, yet starts to roll,
Chasing a lazy squirrel's stroll.
With every bite, a silly sound,
Of crunch and giggle all around!

Musing on a Branch's Edge

On a branch, a wise old crow,
Shares all secrets, tales, and woe.
He caws of risks for nuts and seeds,
Enthusiastic chats with buzzing bees.

A turtle grins in nearby shade,
Wishing he could join the parade.
With every laugh that fills the air,
Nature's giggles are everywhere!

The Stillness of Gathering Clouds

Beneath the fluff of cotton skies,
The squirrels gather, plotting their heists.
A fruit thief drops his tasty prize,
While birds gossip about who bites the best.

Lemonade flows in a shady spree,
Laughter bursts like ripe cherries pop.
A kid swings high, higher than a bee,
Noticing this, the lemonade takes a flop.

Now clouds drift by, tossing silly hats,
A lazy dog joins in with a yawn.
What mischief lies in those fluffy chaps?
Perhaps a rain dance by the early dawn.

So we all gaze at the whims of fate,
Dreaming of pies and a grand, juicy feast.
In the calm before the giggly debate,
The clouds wait patiently, to say the least.

Where Sun and Shade Converse

Between the dance of sun and shade,
A tomato blushes, feeling quite coy.
A rabbit hops, making a parade,
Chasing shadows with glee and joy.

A breeze teases the leaves' gentle tune,
While ants debate a map for a feast.
Under the sun, day turns to June,
Where laughter lives and time is the least.

The bees wear tiny hats, what the buzz!
With nectar plans that would make one cheer.
While worms tell tales of wondrous fuzz,
Under a sunbeam, a giggle appears.

Silly as laughter, so light and bright,
The flowers nod, knowing the game.
As sun and shade whisper day and night,
Each moment felt, nothing's the same.

The Symphony of Swaying Stems

In this garden of giggles and bloom,
We dance along to a humming tune.
Where daisies sway, dispelling our gloom,
And bumblebees sport hats 'neath the moon.

A tomato jokes with a neighboring sprout,
As the sun giggles, stretching its rays.
With every wind, laughter spins about,
The stems sway gently in nature's ballet.

A scarecrow dreams of a not-so-unique,
While crickets chirp in harmonious rhyme.
The carrots discuss the weather next week,
Wishing they'd catch a break from their grime.

So here we bounce, a merry brigade,
With each step comes a skip, a delight!
In this rhythmic place, never to fade,
We sway and dance till the fall of night.

An Odyssey Among Green Shadows

A cucumber rolls and a radish spins,
Through leafy lanes where mischief sits.
A lettuce laughs as it tickles the twins,
While peas just chatter, sharing their wits.

The sun winks down, plotting surprise,
As shadows frolic in playful chase.
A ladybug dons its fun disguise,
And a spider practices its silly grace.

With every step, a story unfolds,
Of whispers, giggles, and joy in the air.
A pumpkin dreams, its destiny bold,
While telling roots, "Oh, life is fair!"

Among green shadows, adventures blend,
Where the wise old tree shudders with cheer.
In the dance of nature, all troubles mend,
And the world spins bright without a fear.

Beneath the Canopy of Time

The squirrels gather for a feast,
Their acorns rolled like tiny beasts.
Chasing tails and having fun,
They plan their pranks beneath the sun.

The branches sway, a gentle tease,
As birds chirp loud with utmost ease.
They throw a dance, a feathered show,
While bees buzz by – oh, how they glow!

A raccoon dons a mask, quite bold,
While watching ants carry crumbs of gold.
"Hey here, you clumsy fellows, stop!"
He hollers out, with laughter's plop.

A breeze that tickles leaves so meek,
Whispers secrets that make them squeak.
A riddle told by nature's jest,
This place is home, truly the best!

The Dance of Falling Petals

Petals swirl like tiny kites,
Caught in plays of sunny lights.
A ladybug spins with glee,
Eager to join the jubilee.

The flowers laugh, they twist and sway,
In colors bright, they dance and play.
A clumsy bee trips on a stem,
Causing all to smile – oh, gem!

A breeze gives chase; oh such a race!
Tickling noses with its embrace.
"Don't fly too high, you'll lose your cheer!"
The petals shout, but never fear.

As evening falls, the frogs will croak,
They swap their tales with every joke.
With moonlit smiles, the night takes part,
In laughter's rhythm, joy and art.

Silent Guardians of Green

The trees wear crowns of vibrant green,
While gnomes play hide-and-seek unseen.
They chuckle low, they giggle loud,
Pretending to be shy, not proud.

The shadows stretch, they tease and creep,
As crickets chirp; it's time for sleep.
A squirrel dons a wizard's hat,
Enchanting friends with tales of chat.

Under leaves, secrets unfold,
Like mischief whispered, brave and bold.
A snail complains, "This path is slow!"
Yet finds joy in every so-called woe.

The murmurs of the night, they jest,
As fireflies dance, their light a quest.
Together here, they share their cheer,
In nature's arms, so warm and clear.

In the Whispering Lattice

The vines entwine with jokes to share,
A melody drifts through the air.
The groundhog sings, a one-hit tune,
While shadows dance beneath the moon.

A pumpkin grins, quite round and proud,
Echoes laughter from the crowd.
With tiny feet, the mice will prance,
Beneath the leaves, they whirl and dance.

The owls hoot tales of yore,
Of silly cats and so much more.
They ponder wise, but fail to see,
A wedged-up dog, stuck in a tree.

As twilight falls, the chorus grows,
And through the leaves, the laughter flows.
In whispers shared, the magic's clear,
In nature's folly, joy draws near.

The Enchantment of Twilight Groves

On a branch, a squirrel pranced,
Wearing acorns like a crown.
He danced near the apples' glance,
While bees played hopscotch down.

A rabbit gave a wink,
As he juggled ripe pears.
His fluffy tail made me think,
Who knew these woods had flares?

Caterpillars sang in choir,
With tongues wrapped 'round a stem.
They dreamed of skies on fire,
While I just swayed with them.

Underneath that bough's embrace,
Laughter filled the air,
The fruits joined in the race,
Chasing clouds without a care.

The Breath of the Fruitful Earth

Where plump berries play hide-and-seek,
A gopher blushes in the shade.
With every rustle, the laughter's peak,
As tomatoes are on parade.

Watermelons whisper gossip,
In the language of seeds and vines.
Eggplants twirl, they just won't stop,
Painting tales in tangy lines.

A parrot dropped an orange,
Splattering juice like confetti.
The ground soaked in the strange derange,
Ancient laughter—the first confetti.

As critters gather all around,
They share a wiggly dance,
In nature's fun, they proudly bound,
With a fruit-filled, froggy prance.

Comfort Under the Leafy Sky

A sunbeam wraps around my feet,
As the ants hold a parade.
Grasshoppers jump to the beat,
While we nibble fruit—we won't fade.

A worm played chess with a beetle,
Their rivalry's a silly sight.
A chicken clucked like a teeter,
As she watch from her perch in delight.

Under leaves, the laughter swirls,
With shadows dancing on the ground.
A picnic spreads, and joy unfurls,
With every bite, more fun is found.

Gathered here in playful respite,
Nature's comedy shines bright,
As giggles escalate to flight,
And friendship blooms in brilliant light.

Haikus of the Hidden Grove

Fruit tugs on branches,
A crow tries to lift a peach—
Gossip in the breeze.

Cheeky rabbits hop,
Wearing hats made of lettuce,
Fashion's finest joke.

Grass tickles my toes,
While the sun winks through the leaves—
Nature's playful grin.

A frog croaks a tune,
Conducting cows at sunset—
Evening's giggle blooms.

Where the Nightingale Sings

Under leaves, a chirp and flap,
A nightingale avoids a trap.
It struts with pride, so very bold,
While a squirrel watches, tale untold.

He poses sweet, then makes a song,
A fluffed-up critter, proud and strong.
But then he slips, with quite a flair,
To land, it seems, right in mid-air!

The trees just laugh, the breeze does tease,
While flowers giggle, shaking knees.
With every note, the humor brings,
A jester's dance where nature sings.

So if you hear that raucous tune,
Remember the nightingale's cartoon.
For in the shade where laughter grows,
Even the starlit night bestows.

Realm of Sheltered Resilience

Among the branches, snug and tight,
A little mouse keeps out of sight.
He tells a tale of clumsy cats,
While sipping dew from tiny vats.

The figs above, they wink and sway,
As if to say, "We'll save the day!"
The grounded critters peek and pry,
While dreaming of a pie to fly.

A woodpecker taps with a silly beat,
Declaring all the snacks he'll eat.
Oh, the uproar in this leafy place,
Is filled with joy and funny grace.

In this realm where laughter reigns,
Life's little quirks are never chains.
Resilience dwells, so quirky and bright,
In tales of joy that take to flight.

Dappled Light and Matured Fragrance

Sunlight dances, casting glee,
Citrus scents float wild and free.
A bee buzzes, with a silly hum,
While chubby ants begin to strum.

They gather round with snacks galore,
Though it's a struggle, what a chore!
While cucumbers burst with fruity cheer,
Their antics crack up every ear.

The shadows play tricks, so very sly,
With dancing leaves that wave goodbye.
An apple tumbles, rolls, and spins,
A fruit contest—whoever wins!

From dappled light, to fragrance sweet,
Nature's laughter can't be beat.
For every bite and every giggle,
There's a joyful dance, a silly wiggle!

Tales of the Twisting Trunks

The trees gather round, gossip and chat,
Whispering secrets beneath their hat.
One trunk says, "I've been up to tricks,
Had a dance-off with a bunch of sticks!"

"Oh please," chuckles the branch nearby,
"Your roots dug deep; don't be shy!"
"It's true," replies with a chuckle and grin,
While a wandering snail makes a spin.

Every twist holds a funny tale,
Of wind's wild pranks that never fail.
As shadows swirl and laughter flies,
Nature's playground, fun in disguise.

So heed the whispers when you stroll,
For each twisted trunk hides a funny soul.
In the shade of green, the laughter clings,
Concealing joy in all the things!

Enchanted by the Fruiting Breeze

Beneath the trees, the laughter flies,
As squirrels play hide and seek with pies.
A parrot squawks in a fruity tone,
While bees buzz round like they own a throne.

A peach slipped down, I dodged and spun,
It rolled so far, I'd thought it won.
With arms outstretched, I made a grab,
But tripped and fell—oh, what a blab!

The apples giggled on their bough,
While I lay there, unsure how.
The plums turned red from laughter's clasp,
As I sat stunned, a peach in grasp.

Yet as I rose, all gave a cheer,
These fruit-filled friends brought me good cheer.
For laughter's found where shadows play,
In breezy games of a sunny day.

Reflections in the Shade

A pear once claimed it could outshine,
The grapes that hung, all in a line.
They squabbled fiercely by the well,
As shadows watched and chewed their gel.

The tomatoes blushed at gossip's tale,
While radishes leaned, turned a pale.
In this debate of fruity pride,
I couldn't help but chuckle wide.

From leafy greens, the whispers spread,
An eggplant crowned with a leafy head.
With laughter sweet, they sang their song,
In this leafy shade where they belong.

Yet all was calm at the end of the day,
As sunlight warmed, and games gave way.
Nobody plucked the fruity crown,
As twilight wore a funny frown.

Nestled Among the Roots

Down in the roots, a grape's guard said,
"No feet allowed, just roll in bed!"
A carrot danced, with a wiggly turn,
While onions plotted a fragrant burn.

A dancing beet slipped, oh what a sight,
As he tumbled down in the soft moonlight.
The whispers teased with playful cheer,
"My turn next!" shouted a bulbous sphere.

In rows they squabbled, all in jest,
Beneath the soil, this rooty fest.
A squash said, "Please, do pass the glaze,"
As all the veggies laughed in a daze.

With twists and turns, they grew so bold,
In a world where roots can easily fold.
They shared their secrets, all was fine,
Among the roots where daylight shines.

Silent Stories of the Sylvan

Beneath the boughs where whispers creep,
The berries plot in shadows deep.
A bramble chuckled with a thorny grin,
Declaring victory without a spin.

A fox strolled by, so slick and sly,
Passed by the berries with just a sigh.
"I'm here for fruit, don't you forget!"
The berries giggled, "We'll be your pet!"

With shadows swirling in the clear,
Each fruit revealed their secret cheer.
They shared old tales of sunlit days,
Of antics bold in leafy ways.

Dappled light wove a hilarious dance,
As every fruit took its silly chance.
In sylvan shades, the fun unrolled,
With stories ripe and laughter bold.

Whispers Lost on the Wind

The apples giggle, so round and bright,
While the pears throw parties, all through the night.
Bumblebees dance, with their silly old buzz,
Confusing the ants, all caught in the fuzz.

A squirrel in shades, makes a stylish debut,
He scampers and twirls, like he's in a zoo.
With acorns as maracas, he starts a new craze,
Even the old trees join in with a sway.

The Shade of Ancient Trees

The branches gossip, whispering tales,
Of naughty young sprouts and their clumsy fails.
They laugh at the sun, with their leaf-covered grins,
"You can't catch us now, we're too thick with skins!"

A rabbit hops by, with a curious glance,
Tripping on roots as he tries to dance.
The shade holds secrets, with a flick and a flop,
Turning dull days into a comical chop.

Secrets Cradled in Green

A raccoon jokes, 'What's with all the fuss?'
While munching on berries, he makes quite a mess.
The ferns create laughter with their swaying,
As squirrels toss acorns, in wild dismaying.

Under thick leaves, the sunbeams sneak,
Tickling the bumbles that giggle and squeak.
The grasshoppers tease, in their quirky ballet,
While the shadows giggle, delighting in play.

Corners of Earth and Sky

The sky spills colors, in quirky delight,
While petals flutter down, oh what a sight!
Clouds tease the blue, with a fluffy parade,
As the gophers pop up, in a goofy charade.

The sun winks at flowers, with a golden beam,
While chipmunks engage in their silly little scheme.
Creating a ruckus, oh what a blend,
Nature's a circus, with laughter to send.

Glimpses of Golden Twilight

Beneath the boughs where squirrels play,
A raccoon holds court, come what may.
With acorns stacked in quite the heap,
He wears a crown—he's king of sleep!

The sun dips low, the shadows stretch,
A wobbly deer, her weight she fetch.
With legs like spaghetti all askew,
She pirouettes, just to amuse you!

Crickets sing of tasty treats,
While fireflies practice twirls and beats.
A rabbit hops, and then he trips,
Clutching his carrot—or so it slips!

As dusk descends, the laughter swells,
The trees chuckle, weaving spells.
A chorus of whimsy fills the air,
Come join the fun; there's joy to share!

Reflections in Leafy Light

A plump old owl with spectacles bright,
Reads the news by moonlit light.
With every page, he lets out a hoot,
As mice sneak past in shiny boots.

A family of bluebirds starts to squawk,
Dancing in branches like they're at the park.
But one little chick, with a terrible aim,
Whoops! Hit the cat; oh what a shame!

In leafy halls, the laughter ripples,
With cheeky ants wearing little wiggles.
They march in line, but wait, oh dear!
A bug's parade through sod can cheer!

The sun now bows; stars play peekaboo,
With whims and giggles all around too.
Under vines where shadows yawn,
Join the delight; let's laugh till dawn!

Flora's Sweet Soliloquy

Petals gossip as breezes tease,
"Did you see that bee? He's such a tease!"
While daisies giggle, throwing shade,
A tulip trips and claims it's played.

Dandelions puff, a wishful crowd,
"Let's float away; we're feeling proud!"
But one gets stuck—a sticky plight,
His fluffy cap, a kite in flight!

The roses mock with fragrance grand,
"Don't mind the thorns; it's just our brand!"
A prickly joke, they share with glee,
While chrysanthemums just sip their tea!

As petals twirl, the jokes unfold,
In the garden of laughter, stories told.
With every bloom, a whimsical cheer,
Join the flora; the fun draws near!

Serenade of the Silent Grove

At twilight's cue, the crickets play,
With bandit frogs singing away.
A turtle slow with dreams quite grand,
Wants to join but sinks in sand!

A fox slips in with a clever grin,
Planning a party; let the fun begin!
With raccoons serving snacks on a plate,
They toast to mischief; it's never late!

The owls hoot guidance, wise and bright,
While bats perform in the pale moonlight.
The breeze brings whispers, tales rotated,
"Did you hear? The fireflies are elated!"

As night unfolds a mystical spree,
Join the dance; it's wild but free.
In shadowy realms where laughter flows,
The grove echoes with mirth—who knows?

Conversations with the Wind

The wind came by with a giggle,
Said, "Your hat is quite a wiggle!"
I laughed and tossed it in the air,
It flew right into a big bear's hair.

The trees all leaned in to listen,
As I told them tales, their leaves glisten.
A squirrel chuckled, jumping low,
"Your jokes are nuts!" Oh, how they'd flow!

Every gust had a quip to share,
We'd trade puns that filled the fair.
Breezes whispered, rustling leaves,
In this symphony, no one deceives.

So there we sat, beneath the sun,
With wind and humor, we had our fun.
The world was light, hearts intertwined,
In laughter's embrace, we all aligned.

Stillness Overgrown

Amidst the vines, the grass took flight,
A snail chuckled at the sight.
"I'm not slow, just taking time,"
In his shell, he composed a rhyme.

The daisies danced with silly grace,
Saying, "Join us, just in case!"
They held a tea party, with bugs so bold,
And poured sweet nectar, a sight to behold.

A crow cawed out with such delight,
"Who'd like a riddle? Let's ignite!"
While ants played cards beneath a leaf,
Trading laughs, avoiding grief.

The sun set low, the shadows grew,
We waved goodnight to the silly crew.
In this overgrown, wacky scene,
Life thrived on humor, bright and green.

Swaying with the Branches

The branches swayed as if to tease,
Whispering jokes with every breeze.
"Why did the apple join a band?"
"Because it couldn't find a hand!"

A peach played tunes with a cheeky grin,
While neighbors laughed, with ginger gin.
They wobbled and wiggled in a row,
Prioritizing fun, not putting on a show.

A robin perched with a feathered crown,
Said, "What's brighter? Us or the town?"
With every chirp, laughter did swell,
Those branches spun tales, all was well.

So sway we did beneath the sky,
With every chuckle, time would fly.
In this haven of leafy delights,
We danced through days and funny nights.

A Lullaby for the Orchard

Close your eyes, dear fruit-filled friends,
Dream of silliness that never ends.
The moon will giggle, stars will play,
In this orchard, where night turns to day.

The crickets croon a sleepy tune,
While fireflies dance, a glossy boon.
"Why don't we play hide and seek?"
In shadows and smiles, the world is meek.

A sleepy owl hoots with a smirk,
"You think I'm wise? It's just hard work!"
As laughter echoes through the trees,
Whispers of stories ride the breeze.

So snuggle in, and let's be gay,
With bedtime giggles sweeping the gray.
In this embrace, let happiness grow,
As dreams of orchards toss and throw.

Nostalgia of the Nostalgic Orchard

Beneath old branches, full of glee,
A squirrel hosts a grand tea party.
With acorns served on fine china,
The guests just giggle, and oh how they whine!

The fruits are ripe, but how they tease,
A bee in pants, swaying like a breeze.
With honeyed whispers, it takes a chance,
While daisies join in for a boisterous dance.

The melons roll, twirling in fun,
While laughter echoes beneath the sun.
A rabbit boasts, "I can out hop,"
But tripped on grapes and had to stop!

So here's to visions, sweet and spry,
Of days gone by, with a chuckle and sigh.
For in these lanes, we find delight,
Where every fruit plays hide and seek at night.

The Gentle Goodnight of the Trees

The twilight hums a lullaby,
While crickets wear their bowties spry.
The old oak whispers tales of yore,
While ants march home from their daily tour.

A nightingale gets stage fright,
And croons a tune a tad too light.
The stars snicker, twinkling bright,
As branches sway in sheer delight.

The moon's a pumpkin on a float,
While fireflies dress like boats that gloat.
The breeze throws a pillow fight in glee,
And giggles echo between each tree.

Oh, listen close to the rustling leaves,
As every creature, in slumber, weaves.
With dreams of apples, juicy and round,
Goodnight, sweet friends, till morning's found.

A Garden in Quietude

In a patch where flowers play hide and seek,
A gnome's lost his hat, oh what a sneak!
The daisies chuckle, "Good luck with that,"
While frogs jump in to join the spat.

Tomatoes blush beneath the sun,
While cucumbers laugh, thinking it's fun.
The carrots whisper behind closed leaves,
"Let's tell the tale of the thief who weaves!"

A butterfly flutters in a daze,
While bumblebees stumble through their maze.
With buzzing jokes and merry shouts,
The garden's the stage for playful bouts.

So watch the zinnias dance with flair,
As daisies twirl without a care.
In vibrant hues, they share their tales,
Of sunlit hours where laughter prevails.

The Melodies of Fruited Dreams

When apples sing, the world takes pause,
A melodic crunch, well, what an applause!
Berries bop like kids on a spree,
While oranges roll with a zest for glee.

Pineapples sway, thinking they're stars,
While grapes gossip beneath their bars.
The cherries laugh, they can't keep still,
As peaches tease with a cheeky thrill.

They gather at night, for a grand ballet,
With plums in tutus, ready to sway.
The lemon plays piano, sour and sweet,
While the apricots tap dance on their feet.

Oh, in this orchard, dreams take flight,
With fruit-filled tales spun in sheer delight.
So grab a slice of laughter's rhyme,
Where every bite's a joy, sublime!

Secrets of the Sweet Sapling

In the green glade, laughter rings,
A squirrel stole my lunch, what a thing!
With acorns cheerfully he sat,
Nibbling while I chased my hat.

Underneath the leafy dome,
A frog croaked tales of leaving home.
His dreams of flies, oh what a plight,
He hopped away in sheer delight.

Beneath the blossoms, bees all buzz,
They tango 'round, not making a fuzz.
Ada's pie, oh, what a scene,
Sweet and sticky, where's the queen?

The sun dips low, a prankster's glow,
As shadows dance, delightfully slow.
We'll hide from bugs, let giggles reign,
In this sapling's heart, we'll stake our claim.

Twilight in the Grove

At twilight's gate, the fireflies blink,
I tripped on roots, what do you think?
A gopher chuckled from his den,
As I struggled in, no help from friends.

The owls hooted jokes up high,
While shadows stretched, and dreams flew by.
A chatty crow was our late guest,
His commentary, simply the best!

Moonlight painted silly scenes,
Where critters held their evening beans.
Raccoons served snacks with quite the flair,
A banquet fit for woodland fare.

We danced 'neath stars, a wobbly show,
With laughter echoing, row by row.
What a way to end the day,
In this grove, we lose our way.

Memories Plucked from Branches

With breezy whispers, tales unfold,
Of berry hunts and laughs retold.
Bob slipped down, in pinkish goo,
Blushing like those berries too!

A partridge snickered from his perch,
While we slid down with quite the lurch.
The branches swayed, a leafy slide,
We laughed so hard as hope was tied.

We tucked our dreams in tree bark seams,
Among the leaves, we stitched our schemes.
As chubby cheeks caught sunlight's gleam,
We reveled in our sweet daydream.

The season turns, like all good things,
Yet still, we hear the laughter sings.
We'll pluck our memories from the trees,
And stitch the past with breeze-filled ease.

The Dance of Leaves and Light

Among the leaves, the shadows play,
As golden rays make funnies sway.
We twirled with laughter, what a fuss,
A beetle joined our crazy bus!

With every rustle and gentle jive,
The sunbeam waltzed, we all felt alive.
A butterfly burst forth in cheer,
He joined our laughter, bright and clear.

In whirlwinds of colors and joyful shouts,
We spun in circles, let go of doubts.
Ancient trees chuckled, their roots held strong,
While nature's symphony hummed along.

As night creeps in, we slow the beat,
With giggles fading, still, so sweet.
These fleeting moments, pure delight,
The dance of life, in day and night.

The Language of the Seasons

The leaves have gossip, oh so bold,
In whispers of green, and tales retold.
The blooms debate in colors bright,
While roots have secrets not in sight.

The sun plays tag with shadows spry,
While squirrels launch acorns to the sky.
A breeze that giggles, tickles and sways,
Nature's jesters in vibrant displays.

When winter hints at chilly fates,
The buds roll eyes, "Not yet, mate!"
Spring's a prankster, skipping about,
Making flowers bloom with a cheeky shout.

Each season's a clown, a jester divine,
Sharing its jokes with a punchline so fine.
In the rhythm of life, they spin and tease,
Nature's slapstick, a true comic breeze.

Beneath the Trees' Silent Watch

Beneath the trees, on picnic days,
Ants plot schemes in curious ways.
The kids run wild, with laughter loud,
While branches chuckle, leafy and proud.

A squirrel steals sandwiches, feeling so sly,
As laughter erupts from the passersby.
Under the boughs where all feels right,
A harmless prank, a frisbee flight.

The sun-drenched grass is a stage so grand,
With funny slips and a speaking hand.
Nature rolls its eyes at our clumsy grace,
It has seen all the laughs in this sacred place.

In this woodland theater, delight on display,
Tree trunks are guardians of our play.
Silent watchers of life's silly tale,
With roots so deep, they can never fail.

Fruits of Time and Memory

From apple to pear, the tales are sweet,
Each juicy bite holds a quirky feat.
Lemon's a joker, with zesty remarks,
While cherries giggle and leave their marks.

Old vines twist like a dancer's spin,
Whispering stories of where they've been.
With every harvest, we laugh and cheer,
Fruits are like friends, close and dear.

Bananas slip in their comical race,
With goofy faces all in one place.
The grapes hold a banquet, laughter rolls loud,
Their wrinkled tales make them ever proud.

With every season, the memories cling,
In the orchard's heart, we dance and sing.
Fruits of laughter, of joy divine,
A comical feast, our hearts intertwine.

Twilight's Embrace in the Grove

As twilight drapes its playful veil,
The fireflies wink, with flickers pale.
Crickets chatter in evening's delight,
While the moon plays peek-a-boo with the night.

Owls hoot softly, sharing their jokes,
While laughter bubbles among the folks.
A gathering hum, a delicious buzz,
In the dimming light, oh, what a fuss!

The trees sway gently with a grin,
Rustling leaves sing the night's sweet hymn.
Every shadow holds a chuckle so bright,
As stars gather 'round for a comic sight.

In this twilight grove, the mirth expands,
With nature's embrace, laughter withstands.
A whimsical close to the day's fun spree,
Under the stars, forever carefree.

Blossoms and Secrets Untold

Beneath the trees, the secrets grow,
Dandelions, they steal the show.
A squirrel sneezes, oh what a sight,
The sun giggles, feeling so bright.

Raindrops dance on leaves so green,
Whispers of mischief, a farmer's dream.
Bees buzzing tunes in a clumsy flight,
Nature's circus, a pure delight.

Cherry trees wear polka dot hats,
As raccoons practice their acrobat's spats.
The wind plays tricks, starts spinning around,
While shadows giggle, without making a sound.

A bunny hops, with style and flair,
Sporting a bowtie, like he doesn't care.
Sweet fruits laugh, their colors so bright,
Sharing their joy under soft twilight.

The Whimsy of Wandering Shadows

Shadows prance in playful glee,
They tickle the grass, just wait and see.
A cat with a hat joins the fun,
Chasing the sunlight till the day is done.

The ducks are singing a silly song,
As they waddle along, where they don't belong.
A tree's got jokes, its branches sway,
While squirrels laugh and throw acorns away.

Small shadows hide behind the pears,
Making silly faces, spinning in pairs.
A gopher wears shades, looking quite cool,
While the flowers burst into laughter at school.

Bumblebees dance in the summer air,
Buzzing and whirling, without any care.
The sun beams wide, a clown in disguise,
While grapes gossip in clusters, full of surprise!

Mosaic of Fruits and Dreams

Apples play tag with the sun-kissed breeze,
Oranges giggle, drop down from trees.
Bananas peel laughter, a slippery prank,
As everyone gathers, their spirits rank.

A melon juggles with curious flair,
While cherries giggle without any care.
Lemons quip, sour faces abound,
All while a cantaloupe rolls on the ground.

The strawberry siblings engage in a fight,
Splatting each other, what a funny sight!
Pears chuckle softly, hiding their grins,
At the jesterly antics of fruits with skins.

Dreams of fruit pies fill the warm air,
While the rhubarb polishes its shiny flair.
Clouds drift above, in a whimsical race,
As laughter erupts in this fruity space!

Harmonies of the Orchard's Heart

In the grove, a harmony plays,
Birds chirping tunes on sunny days.
A goat on a hillbelting out a sound,
While the bees buzz along, rounding the ground.

The drum of the woodpecker taps on a tree,
Creating a rhythm, wild and free.
As apples bounce, in a dance of delight,
And pears sway, laughing into the night.

Cherries keep time with their jolly beat,
While the daisies clap with tiny feet.
The breeze joins in, with a whoosh and a sigh,
As shadows leap out, reaching for the sky.

The sun takes a bow, as night starts to creep,
While whispers of stars begin to leap.
Under the moon, the orchard sings on,
A waltz of joy, until the dawn.

The Quiet Harvest's Embrace

Where squirrels juggle acorns high,
And buzzing bees in bow ties fly,
The apples roll, oh what a sight,
Hoping to join the juggling flight.

The farmer naps beneath the sun,
While chickens plot a wobbly run,
They dream of eggs, but what a mess,
A feathered ballet in the dress.

Carts are parked, but who needs wheels?
When melon balls make better meals,
With laughter ripe upon the vine,
We feast on fruit and sip on wine.

So raise a toast to silly things,
Like prancing goats who wear bling-bling,
In fields where joy and laughter grow,
The harvest's more than just a show.

Shadows of Ripening Dreams

Underneath the shady broad,
A stack of pumpkins look like trod,
Each one with a grin, oh what a case,
A jack-o'-lantern's laughing face.

The pears conspire in a dance,
With watermelons taking a chance,
They twirl and jiggle, round and round,
While laughter bounces off the ground.

Tomatoes hide in leafy beds,
Pretending they're asleep instead,
But every laugh, they can't resist,
And start to giggle, pull a twist.

So here's to dreams that tickle us,
With giggles flung, oh what a fuss,
Those shadows dancing in the light,
Make every harvest day a delight.

Echoes Amongst the Trees

When apples whisper, seeds get bold,
With cider jokes that never grow old,
The branches creak, a funny tune,
As secrets float by on a balloon.

A gopher plays tag with a vine,
While sunflowers sip on sweet sunshine,
The shadows dance and laugh with glee,
As every fruit becomes a spree.

A duck in boots, oh what a sight,
Tripping over roots in pure delight,
The leaves all chuckle, join the spree,
In the great green circus of the tree.

So here's to nature's funny games,
With giggles sprouting, never tamed,
In every echo that we hear,
We gather laughter, year by year.

Beneath the Apple Blossom Sky

In a meadow bursting with smiles,
Where daisies chat and gossip for miles,
The blooms are blushing, not quite shy,
As bees buzz by with a playful sigh.

Chickens wear hats, oh what a show,
While ducks debate on which way to go,
Each fruit a joke, they start to fling,
While laughter rings like a bell's sweet ding.

Grapes tumble down from their lofty height,
Performing somersaults in the bright sunlight,
The wind carries giggles on the breeze,
As everyone chuckles beneath the trees.

Raise your glass to the silly and bright,
Harvesting joy in the soft twilight,
In every petal, in every laugh,
The day is a silly, joyful portrait.

The Pearls of Evening Shade

Beneath the trees, a sneaky cat,
Chasing fireflies, as rodents scat.
A squirrel tosses acorns with flair,
While I just try to comb my hair.

An old dog snoozes without a care,
Dreams of chasing a dancing hare.
The breeze whispers jokes to the leaves,
Laughter echoes, and lightly weaves.

Ponderings on a Windy Path

I walked a path where whispers roam,
Chasing thoughts that feel like foam.
A butterfly lands on my nose,
As the tickling music of nature flows.

Curly winds bring giggles galore,
I trip on roots, and call for more.
The flowers chuckle, swaying in time,
While bees bloom with a buzz and rhyme.

Reverie in Leafy Surrounds

The sun peeks through with a playful grin,
Leaves dance around like they're in spin.
I join the laughter of bright blooms,
As bees hum tunes from nature's rooms.

A hedgehog rolls by, a curious sight,
Taking a stroll—oh, what a delight!
The trees throw shade like a cozy quilt,
While my sandwich escapes, quite the guilt.

Hidden Sanctuaries of Calm

Beneath the boughs where shadows play,
A picnic's here to brighten the day.
Sandwiches tumble, ants hold their feast,
As I laugh at the chaos, to say the least.

The sunbeams sparkle, a cheeky show,
Dancing with laughter, as if to throw.
A pair of frogs leap, vying for fame,
As the pink buttercups giggle their name.

Echoes of a Sundrenched Day

Beneath the branches, laughter spills,
Where squirrels trade their acorn drills.
A bee buzzes with a cheeky grin,
As if to say, let the games begin!

The sun laughs loud, a golden crown,
As shadows stretch and twirl around.
A picnic spread with crumbs and jam,
And ants performing for the fam!

Secrets Unraveled in Green

A hidden hawk with a wink so sly,
Watches a rabbit hop and fly.
They swap their tales of daring feats,
While munching on some fruity treats.

The grass giggles underfoot,
As shoes get stuck, oh what a hoot!
A worm does a dance, quite absurd,
While a nearby cat just stares, disturbed.

Nature's Hidden Conversations

The trees whisper secrets in the breeze,
While daisies nod to the buzzing bees.
A frog croaks jokes from his lily pad,
Making sure the snails aren't too sad.

Clouds gossip about passing trains,
As children chase their colorful planes.
A twist of fate, a slip, a slide,
Nature giggles wide, can't hide!

When Time Stands Still

A moment frozen, laughter rings,
As kids play tag, and the rule book flings.
A goat chews grass, with a cheeky stare,
While a bird drops a joke mid-air.

The sun winks softly, dusk draws near,
The world slows down, but not in fear.
With every chuckle, time takes a pause,
In nature's arms, without a cause.

A Canopy of Time

Beneath the branches, squirrels run,
Chasing each other, having fun.
A picnic basket, all things sweet,
But ants decide to crash the feast.

The apples giggle in the breeze,
Trying hard not to lose their leaves.
A pair of birds, they laugh and sing,
As butterflies cheer, 'Let's do our thing!'

A long-lost shoe lies in the grass,
Who knew it could be such a class?
With every tree, a story unfolds,
Of mischief and laughter, a treasure untold.

As day turns to night, shadows sway,
The stars peek out to join the play.
While crickets chirp, they stomp and dance,
Oh, what a night, let's take a chance!

Fragments of Sun and Shade

In the dappled light where giggles grow,
Sunbeams tickle, to and fro.
A lemon's face, so bright and round,
Makes all the melons spin around.

The bees all buzz a silly tune,
While plums debate how to moonwalk soon.
Ripe cherries pout, all dressed in red,
Wishing for crowns upon their head.

The shadows stretch and stretch some more,
As fruit flies hold a silly war.
Over the strawberries, heads collide,
But laughter wins, as they confide.

The sun dips low; day becomes night,
Fruits and critters hold on tight.
A firefly brings the final cheer,
With chuckles and giggles, we end the year!

The Stillness Between Fruits

A pause hangs thick in the warm air,
As the pears practice their best stare.
Plums roll around, trying to tease,
While peaches plot their next grand squeeze.

The shadow of a cat lingers near,
With thoughts of a snack and a sneaky leer.
Banana slips make for a silly fall,
As oranges bounce, embracing it all.

The stillness breaks with a great loud clap,
As everyone turns to take a nap.
But the shadows chuckle, making a game,
Whispering tales that never quite came.

In the quiet, stories brew,
Of mischief that no one knew.
With laughter wrapped in evening's cloak,
A sleepy hush over every folk.

Lullabies of the Leafy Isles

In leafy nooks where whispers play,
Fruits and nuts decide to sway.
A berry boisterously tells a joke,
About a nut that thought he'd croak.

The fig wore shades, so very sly,
While limes debated the meaning of pie.
Cherries chime in with a sweet refrain,
Singing of sunshine, rain, and rain.

The wind brings tales from far away,
Of adventures the ripe ones wouldn't say.
As squirrels join in with their little pots,
To stir up giggles and buttery knots.

Even twilight dances in delight,
As the leaves sway and stars ignite.
All together, they hum and cheer,
For the lullabies we hold so dear!

Solace Amongst the Leaves

The squirrel's dance upon the boughs,
A nutty dream of simple browse.
With acorns dropped like little bombs,
He shakes his tail, and then he calms.

The rabbits plot their leafy heist,
While birds gossip, oh aren't they nice!
With funny hats that flowers wear,
They laugh and twirl without a care.

The sunbeams giggle through the trees,
While shadows play with whispers, please.
Each leaf a secret, soft and shy,
They share their tales as breezes sigh.

So here we sit, amidst this cheer,
With nature's antics drawing near.
In laughter's arms, we find our glee,
Under the leaves, so wild and free.

Shadows of Ripening Dreams

The pears are plotting their escape,
In checkered patterns, dressed like tape.
They giggle as they start to fall,
A juicy prank, a fruity squall.

The breeze tickles through tomato vines,
As herbs gossip in silly lines.
With every breeze, a laugh is spread,
While ladybugs perform instead.

The strokes of sunlight paint the ground,
As ants march in, a busy sound.
They dance and prance, their tiny feet,
To make a rhythm oh-so-sweet.

As shadows shift, the chuckles bloom,
Nature's stage, devoid of gloom.
With ripening dreams about to burst,
We laugh aloud, for joy's a must.

Beneath the Canopy's Embrace

Beneath the leaves, we find a chair,
Where all the giggles drift in air.
The beetles race with tiny hats,
While munching blooms and talking spats.

The sunbeams tease the ripened fruit,
As longing eyes pursue the loot.
They sway and sway with every breeze,
And make us smile, oh yes, they tease!

The shadows stretch, a playful guise,
That tickles us and makes us rise.
To join the fun, to dance around,
With nature's circus all profound.

So here we sit, beneath this bliss,
In laughter's hold, we find our kiss.
With each sweet moment spent in glee,
Nature's charm is wild and free.

Echoes of Sunlit Paths

On paths where sunbeams chase their friends,
We wander through where laughter bends.
With every step, a funny sound,
As silly tales come whirling 'round.

The butterflies, in boisterous flight,
Swap jokes of love, oh what a sight!
While daisies giggle, stand-up blooms,
With sunny faces in the rooms.

A gopher peeks with a cheeky grin,
As he rolls out, the game begins!
With quick little hops and winks so sly,
He steals the show, oh my oh my!

Amongst the echoes of our play,
Each tiny laugh brightens the day.
With friendships forged in nature's light,
We find our peace, our hearts take flight.

www.ingramcontent.com/pod-product-compliance
Lightning Source LLC
Chambersburg PA
CBHW051630160426
43209CB00004B/582